OVERCOMING

SCATTERED

SHADOWS

Conquer your Fear, Succeed, and Win

KRISTI R COWAN

OVERCOMING SCATTERED SHADOWS

Conquer your Fear, Succeed, and Win

Published by Kristi R. Cowan

Copyright © 2022 by Kristi R. Cowan
ISBN Print: 978-0-578-36049-2
ISBN eBook: 978-0-578-36048-5

The author reserves all rights to this book. They do not permit anyone to reproduce or transmit any part of this book through any means or form, be it electronic or mechanical. No one also has the right to store the information herein in a retrieval system. Neither do they have the right to photocopy, record copies, scan parts of this document, etc., without the publisher's or author's proper written permission.

Disclaimer

All the information in this book will be used only for informational and educational purposes. The author will not account for any results that stem from using the contents herein. While conscious and creative attempts have been made to ensure that all information provided herein is as accurate and useful as possible, the author is not legally bound to be responsible for any damage caused by the accuracy and use/misuse of this information.

Every attempt has been made to source all quotes properly.
Cover Art: Kim Cowan
Cover Design: Kim Cowan
Formatting and Interior Design: Brandon Evans
First Edition 2022
Printed in the United States of America

Dedication

To All the People in My Life, Who Helped Me Overcome: Parents - Alicia & JW, Sister- Kimberly.

To my Children, Kamer'n & Kristen, Who Are Dear to My Heart and My Reason Why.

Table of Contents

Introduction 1

Chapter One: Overcoming The Shadow of a Doubt 5

Chapter Two: Overcoming Family Obstacles 12

Chapter Three: Overcoming Relationship Issues 18

Chapter Four: Overcoming Friend Dilemmas 22

Chapter Five: Overcoming Negativity 26

Chapter Six: Overcoming The Past 31

Chapter Seven: Overcome To Become 35

Introduction

Challenges are inevitable realities of life. Everyone born of a woman must face their fair share of life's travails. The success stories we celebrate in all walks of life are men and women who have learned to turn defeat into victories, failure into success, and gains from past pain.

Thomas Edison, who invented the electric bulb, failed 999 times before getting it right on the 1000th try. When asked what kept him going all those times of failure upon failures, he said, "Those 999 times of failures show 999 ways of not making the electric bulb." Perception in life is everything.

Some twenty years back, I had to realize this fact. I chose to forgive the younger version of myself and let go of past wrong choices and decisions to make the best of the adult I was becoming.

Another major life lesson I received from my varied experiences is to be careful with my time and effort in others when it is not mutually beneficial. You must ensure you take care of yourself and be unapologetic about it.

This book is about bouncing back when life's punches throw you down. Standing tall with trembling legs and burning arms. It is my life story and a testament to anyone who can relate. And anyone who needs to hear this:

It is okay to be confident, to speak your mind, and make aware that there is nothing wrong with being yourself. It is good to have goals different from the popular opinions of family, friends, and peers.

Let go of toxicity that would drain you of your joy, peace, happiness, and energy. Break away from abuse of all kinds; emotional, verbal, and physical.

This is me giving you a raw synopsis of good experiences and not-so-good experiences and how I overcame various shades of challenges, hoping to help others through any mistakes and choices, both right and wrong.

If I can turn my stumbling blocks into stepping stones, so can you.

OVERCOMING SCATTERED SHADOWS

Chapter One

Overcoming The Shadow of a Doubt

I was always passionate about writing. As a young girl, I loved to put my thoughts and creations on paper. The idea that this was all I had to do to bring my ideas to life excited me, even more, when another person could read what I wrote. A true comfort had buried itself within the lines of the page. I started by writing short poems that were appealing to the younger crowd, and as I got older my passion for writing got stronger, and my poems started to expand their horizons. These things got me into the performing arts in high school, which further fueled the fire that sparked within me to burst into creation.

However, at one point in my life, that flame had snuffed out at the hands of the critic that lived in my mind.

Apart from my cousin, who wrote a few books, I was the only writer in the family. I never really mentioned my passion for writing to anyone except for the family closest to me because I had plenty of ideas, but I struggled to mold them together into my very own work. It was draining for teenage me, revisiting a piece repeatedly, trying to correct the little things I saw so wrong with it. It never seemed to end. I thought, after all, I would not make a career out of writing, it ended up succumbing to simply a hobby.

Eventually, I pushed writing to the side completely, whenever I wrote, I kept it to myself.

This cycle continued. My mother observed this change within me. She knew I had a gift, and she was never the one to keep quiet about something. But even as she tried to spark my inspiration again, I felt as if the goal was just out of my grasp.

I plagued my consciousness with "What if?" and I felt I was letting down the people who believed in my dream.

So, I shifted from writing to music at full speed. I sang at churches, school choirs, and small events, participated in various competitions, and proceeded to songwriting using my writing skills. Through another form of art, my writing had finally been reborn.

But my main inspiration to keep my writing alive is my second-born. I saw a lot of myself in her. She loves to write, just like me. She is the one that has inspired me to pursue my old passion because I know for a fact that if she had the resources and experience that I have to offer, then through me she would express that passion I have.

This is the mindset you must set for yourself. Figure out the why in your goals and dreams. If you want to achieve these milestones, you have to develop a productive mindset. Set checkpoints, sweat in your efforts, and be patient with yourself.

At some point, I felt content with life. I got everything I could ever need from my parents who loved me very much. I gained a sister and the possibility of being a role model for someone who would look up to me. I wanted to be a worthy example. However, this came with a lot of unneeded worries and self-doubt.

I held back a lot growing up because of this worry. Being the oldest, I was not the one being pushed, I was the pusher.

On careful analysis, I realized that another major cause of my self-doubt came from negative experiences throughout my life. Relationship struggles, disrespect, feelings of helplessness, feelings of failure, and pressure on others' expectations. I felt undeserving and had moments where I thought that bringing attention to myself would make all of these unwanted feelings fade.

I began losing track of what my strengths are as my own person. I gravitated to the attention and began depending on how it made me feel at that moment.

I allowed myself to grow by having a better plan that was perfect for me. For example, Listen to yourself - What does your heart tell you?

Trust that instinct, whether it is a hobby you want to incorporate or a career you want to start. It is great and helpful to get advice from others, but you shouldn't base your life on what others think is best for you. Do what feels right, Be true and comfortable with yourself. Be grateful for what you have.

I am sure you have heard the saying "Don't Judge a Book by Its Cover."

It is very common, and it may seem obvious or cheesy, but in your life, you will start to notice how true these common statements are. People may make assumptions and perceive you differently than you are. This is a thing you cannot control. Do not waste time worrying about your image to other people. All that matters is how YOU perceive yourself, it is okay if some people get that perception wrong, because ultimately, their view does not define you.

When I realized this, then the doors started opening.

So, Take pride in yourself! Staying true to your values makes you feel fulfilled. No one has the right to take that from you. When you know that you deserve to be treated right and/or fairly, as a result, you do not tolerate others treating you unfairly. Building your confidence and maintaining healthy relationships with other people throughout your life can be done.

Pen down the qualities you like the most about yourself, think hard, and figure out what you excel at or need to work on. And most importantly: Do not be afraid. One bad try is another fresh start.

Chapter Two

Overcoming Family Obstacles

One of my family members said:
"You're going to be the one that brings the family together."

I did not know what that meant. I was meeting this family member for the first time. However, upon first impression, she felt I was genuine and trustworthy to hold the bond between two separate families. Because of this, I would often ask myself why so many people believe in me. But I never complained when people came to me for help. I get that from my mom. She knows how to put things together and make everything seem okay.

My mom is often the go-to person and is always there to help. Even if she knew that what she was about to take on could be a challenge, she accepts and tackles any and everything that is added to her everyday life. There is one thing that I have noticed about my mom over the years; she is a person that never says "No." Now, this doesn't always correlate with a negative thing but saying "No." can be a form of self-respect by setting boundaries. Being pleasing and easygoing is normalized, so it is all right if you do not master this skill quickly. Give yourself time to grow and realize your problems before you start to tackle them.

I graduated from a fine arts high school but immediately went to college majoring in Biology with a concentration in Physical Therapy. I decided to start college life in Bolivar Missouri, which was about eight hours away from my hometown. I felt out of place at the moment of arrival.

Even so, attending college for the first time changed me in so many ways. College helped me become self-aware, made me more responsible because I was no longer under my parents' wing, and helped me shape my independence.

During the time of my first encounter with college, there were a lot of restrictions. There wasn't a very high percentage of African Americans that attended unless they were in sports. And even then, they had to travel many hours away. Moving so far away gave me mixed emotions at first, but the idea of possibly more opportunities to improve my craft and sharpen my skills in the field that I chose was just what I needed to accomplish.

In retrospect, I should have mentioned to my mom that I was not on board with the idea of going to that school, but at the time I thought:

"She's my mom, who am *I* to question her?"

Life took a different turn for me when I was gifted with my first child while going to college. Due to school restrictions, religious regulations, and guidelines, I returned to my hometown for school. I never gave up on my goals and aspirations. I never stopped going to school, but I did have fear and doubt in my mind that I would fail and not achieve what I wanted out of life. Again, I kept all of these thoughts discrete and didn't share them with anyone, just like how I did with my writing. Do not hesitate to experience and try something new because you would never know if you do not experience anything. Grow that ambition to achieve your goals, and practice self-control, especially in difficult situations.

My firstborn is now twenty-three, smart but stubborn, and holds onto things from the past that still affects his life to this day. From my observations and interactions with him, it seemed as if he was always angry as a child. Growing up, his father was not in his life like he wanted him to be.

Even today, it still bothers him; he wants to know where his father is and have a connection and relationship with him, but my son has forced a detachment from anything that reminds him of his childhood, including me. My son and I have not had a relationship for 4 years.

Today, my son now lives out of state. There is no contact between him and me. There are no calls, texts, or even visits from both parties. There is not a day I do not think about my son and hope he is safe and well.

I do hope and pray we will reconnect soon rather than later. In the meantime, I try to keep my focus on my current responsibilities as a mother to my daughter. As a single mother of two, most times I did not have time to focus on my mental well-being. I just knew that if I broke down, I would not be able to take care of my children.

Execute all you can in your children to the best of your ability. To know that your child recognizes and appreciates what you do and have done for them speaks volumes. Your effort and abilities will show.

When my son was brought into the world, we lived in my hometown, and his father lived in another state at the time. There were always promises of being there for our child, but those promises were not fulfilled, and the inconsistency of visits and continuous heartbreaks became stressful.

I knew early in my child's life that I would be left taking on this responsibility alone. However, my son decided he did not need any of his family and sheltered himself from any kind of contact or help.

I have learned from some of the mistakes I made earlier in life, though some of those bad decisions were made with external influence. I decided to entertain those choices, so I had to take full responsibility for my actions.

Part of being young is learning that your life will be filled with trials and tribulations, but it is also a time of your life when you undergo plenty of changes- creating and figuring out your personality.

I would encourage all parents that whenever your child has questions about the absent parent, answer all questions but answer with honesty and be smart about it.

Be kind and keep your feelings out of it. Encourage co-parenting if at all possible. Try to stay positive and be patient with how your child copes but be open to conversations when they are needed. You are their only role model, so anything you do or say, they will do as well. Be vigilant.

Chapter Three

Overcoming Relationship Issues

My relationships affected me in different ways depending on the person and the role that person played in my life. I had great relationships with people, and I had those not-so-great relationships. There were times when I thought the connections, I had would last forever but did not, which affected me for years.

My romantic relationships began around my teenage years. My son was born into this world within a broken home. The bond between a father and son did not exist which created a missing piece that I could not fulfill. My daughter was born later. Yet again, another child was brought into the world that experienced that absence and disconnect from a parent. So, I was left to figure it out. I became emotionally damaged in a sense because of the verbal abuse which led to a lack of self-esteem.

I was left with a lot of responsibility before I was ready, so I had to grow up quickly. I was raised well and gained that strong woman energy from my mom and that sense of who I am from my dad, so there I was a single mother with two children, a couple of jobs, and going to school all at once. Even if I did not feel strong at times, I knew those children of mine could not and would not know how weak and selfless I felt.

I believe everyone that has dated at some point has had those relationships that are unforgettable. You give your heart, then it is shattered due to some form of lack of communication, lack of respect, a difference in priorities, loss of trust, and even falling out of love. You start to question yourself when it has happened more than once. Future relationships may suffer due to this baggage. I began to lose myself and forget who I was.

Those that I thought loved me were extremely critical. Ongoing stressful life events such as failed relationships and traumatic experiences broke me down. Me boxing away my feelings was probably the worst thing I could have done. It takes a toll on your physical and mental state.

I figured putting my feelings away in what I felt was a safe place and dealing with them later was the best thing to do at the moment. Painful feelings that have not been addressed can replay over and over again in your head. Discover your coping strategy and express it!

Other relationships throughout my adult life, good or bad, taught me life lessons; for instance: Choose your emotional state, The moments of pain are worth all the joy, People are capable of change, The past can only affect you if you let it, Learn to compromise, Forgiveness is powerful, Love can change over time.

I had to learn that my imperfections and mistakes teach us what does not work and encourage us to create new ways of thinking and doing and that mistakes are proof that we are trying. We are trying things that we may be afraid of. Things that may make us feel uncomfortable. Things that we thought were good for us or that we thought we wanted. We have to move past the loss and possible embarrassment. Mistakes will make you feel like you are a failure, but what we often do not realize is that failures are packed with blessings; which will open countless pools of amazing things and opportunities.

You can discover yourself before getting into any relationship to avoid losing that sense of independence. You are capable of anything. If you find yourself lost or stuck in any situation, take a long hard look, and find yourself again. Remember how you got there, reconnect with yourself, and love yourself again. Remember what you love to do and go do it. Expand your comfort zone regularly, whether that is in a relationship, reconnection with loved ones, career path, or taking a leap of faith in a dream that you always wanted in your life.

Remember you have the power to be, have, and do anything you desire. No one can predict your future but you sure can create it.

Chapter Four

Overcoming Friend Dilemmas

I had friends that I grew up with from the church. They were my home away from home. And they felt the same way because they always came to me for advice.

Though I was there for everybody else, nobody, ever asked:

"Are you okay?"

Because of this, I was left to consider everyone else's feelings and not my own.

When I got older, I had the opportunity to make some decisions on my own, just like everyone else. I had to decide who was friend worthy. You have to weigh your pros and cons so you can reflect on your friendships over the past few days, weeks, months, and/or years.

I sometimes see myself as different in some crowds depending on the things, I am into. I realized that I needed to be around people that were like me. I had friends who could relate to what I was doing. The older me did not do anything that was way out of the ordinary, but I always had thoughts that something was missing. As a teen, I knew that I had not experienced real life. But as an adult, I considered myself as well beyond my years.

I thought of a way that made me stick out from the crowd; like cracking a bunch of jokes to maintain my relevancy. Thinking back, this was a distraction from my wandering brain.

I was a people pleaser. I always wanted and needed to get better "content" to make people notice me. I felt like if I made five people happy today, I have to make ten happy tomorrow. I thought that my value depended on whether or not I was on someone's mind.

I was accepting of everyone and was told repeatedly that they feel inexplicably comfortable around me. Unfortunately, acquaintances, friends, close friends, and best friends come and go in and out of your life. I had to realize that hiding your vulnerability does not make us more likable, just a little more noticeable. I hated the fact that some of my friendships did not last. I blamed it all on myself, but some friendships are meant to be repaired and some are not. I am a stickler for repairing what was not meant to be broken.

Repairing a friendship can be difficult and stressful to achieve depending on the situation that caused it to decline. Repairing can include choosing a different way to communicate. Give it time and try again if you see fit. We all change over time so circumstances and priorities will change as well.

Be open and flexible to those changes. In all actuality do not ignore the red flags because you cannot fix what does not want to be fixed or what is not meant to be fixed. But your friends have boundaries too, and in the same way that you want to be respected, you should do the same for them.

I put on a new personality outside of college. Though I still cared about how people perceived me, I was less concerned about getting attention. I just did things that supported the perception I was trying to create. I did that with my personality and appearance because my mom had always told me to dress in certain ways when going out in public. I tried to blend in with every environment or situation in which I found myself because that is all I knew.

Now people who knew me from college see me as a changed person. I see that as a good thing. I was not just adapting; I was evolving. I refused to get stuck in the cage of my life. I instead focused on the positive and left my comfort zone.

There was much consideration when I decided to change my residence, I would feel alone, but at the same time, I would learn to form new relationships and become self-sufficient. Throughout my life, I have discovered myself. My Life experiences influenced my thoughts, feelings, and behaviors, and shaped my personality traits.

Chapter Five

Overcoming Negativity

I often felt there was a lot of negativity in my life at times. I felt like I was being punished for something, but I could not figure out what that something was and why. After several years, I found a way to deal with those negative thoughts that were lingering in my mind. I started to focus on helping someone else. Helping someone else allowed me to bring positivity into my life. Whether it was physically helping someone or just being a listening ear, was in actuality my therapy. Your goals can provide aid in other areas as well.

I would tell anyone that finds themselves in an uncomfortable situation to - put it all out on the table. For you to be there for someone else or feel whole as a person, someone needs to know how you feel.

Try to see some good in every situation and handle it from there; but if it feels like you can't get anything across, you can't help the issue at hand, or you feel like you don't have your voice or opinion in the situation, you have to excuse yourself.

I have been in so many situations, from verbal abuse to emotional abuse, because I stayed silent. It takes confidence to move away from any situation.

There were times when I felt like the negativity in my life was at an all-time high. My involvement included people I had a close connection to that treated me with the utmost disrespect. There were times I was called out by my name. There were times that I experienced domestic abuse. There were times when I was constantly reminded that I did not matter.

I was threatened at times and was taken advantage of because I was labeled as weak by them. I was distraught after so much mistreatment that I developed trust issues and anxiety.

I had to learn to simmer myself down; it took a lot of willpower to create this unapologetic woman. I trained my brain to think more positively even though I went through some trauma in my life. I also allowed support from family, friends, and specialists when needed.

I was tempted to internalize all the trauma. I often questioned myself and tried to see what I needed to change. I even tried to get confirmation from those that were closest to me. Obtaining this confirmation was not a way to put all blame on oneself, but it sets you one step ahead.

Everybody is strong in their own way, and once the confidence is there, that is a reminder to yourself of your capabilities. If your confidence is not quite there, try to challenge yourself. First get outside of your comfort zone because you will discover things, that you didn't know you were, Set a new goal, Learn about something, Wake up earlier in the morning to incorporate exercise or meditation, or reach out to someone that inspires you or someone you look up to, Stay away from social media and/or electronics for a while, Set a savings goal, Write in a journal,

Reconnect with an old friend, Travel, get rid of a bad habit, make a new friend, or create a vision board.

These are all hobbies or activities that will help you cope while also giving you a new skill or habit to incorporate into your life. Challenging yourself gives you that confidence in your abilities to be powerful and unstoppable.

Keep your power. When you are around a person(s) with negative energy you can easily permit that person to steal your joy. Make that decision to hold on to yourself and your power and refuse to let the negative person own you.

Stay positive, think positive, and be hopeful. You may have to step away and regroup, find something positive and focus on it, look past your negativity as reassurance that you will not be stuck in this forever Ask for help and guidance, and develop an attitude of gratitude.

Find the good in your life and do not allow another person's miserableness and insecurities to define you. Ignore the offender and remove yourself so you do not fall into the trap with negative energy.

Confront your feelings rather than avoid them. Do not feel that because you have a difference of opinion you do not matter. Find your voice.

OVERCOMING SCATTERED SHADOWS

Chapter Six

Overcoming The Past

My past stuck with me for years, and throughout those years confidence was lost, and it was difficult to express myself. The stress and difficult life events harmed my self-esteem. Through willpower and having a strong mind, I overcame my self-doubt. Knowing that we are our biggest inner critics, I practiced self-compassion by thinking back to past and present achievements. I praised myself for being a great mother to my children. I patted myself on the back for following the goals I set for myself. I spent time with positive supportive people. I did not compare myself to others. I revisited my old passion for journaling and writing into my lifestyle which helped me regulate a lot of my emotions, confidence, and self-identity.

Journaling is my therapy but mostly it is a way to freely express yourself. Traumatic events whether they are small or large can sometimes be hard to cope with. These events can sometimes take control over your life. This does not mean that you have to choose journaling as your coping mechanism, however, to have one in the first place is beneficial. Actions regarding another person such as manipulation are one crucial behavior towards others. Manipulation is a sign of power and can be used as control. My experience through traumatic events whether it was mental or emotional, has taught me that it is okay to question one's motives. Be clear about your perspective and stick to it.

You have the power to protect your peace. No one will care for and guard your physical, mental, emotional, and even spiritual self, more than you.

Protecting your peace is personal and only you can and should set boundaries for yourself. Do not ever be afraid to walk away and setting boundaries and sticking to them will all protect your inner peace.

Recognize that you cannot change other people. You will likely end up being frustrated or in an argument. More times than most I experienced others wanting me to change or be who or how they wanted me to be. My feelings were often not accounted for. In some instances, changing yourself is good for a relationship. It is necessary but it has to be an agreement for change, not something that is forced on another.

A lot of times, we as humans fear change because it means that outcomes are unknown. We panic because we do not know what may happen and then create worry. Pushing yourself to change for the good on your terms is a sign of growth and it will allow you to change some things that you may not like or how you view yourself.

A great way to overcome your past is to have a plan for your life and start working on it. Do not just write it down but start acting on those plans. Let the people in your life know you are up to something, then seize the time you need to get it done without distraction.

Chapter Seven

Overcome To Become

Being your younger self, you have a bright future ahead. So, go for it, and it will better your life and that of people who are connected in one way or the other. There will be obstacles but overcoming those obstacles is what counts.

In my early twenties, I forgave my younger self for things that were not beneficial for my life and just moved forward. The biggest thing I have forgiven myself for is not going for all I wanted to do. I also excused myself for depending on other people for happiness. You are the only one that can make yourself happy.

Once you are older, you will learn that life is not short if you do not live it that way. Adaptation will come with the changes you make.

Your life is all yours so stop living for others and do what is best for you. Stay off your high horse and be humble. Be mature but know when to lighten up, laughter creates happiness. Do not take everything to heart because everyone is not out to get you. It is never too late.

Overcome your limitations by loving yourself. One of the most powerful things I have been doing recently is practicing self-care. Pay attention to your happiness because you can often lose yourself in someone else. Be aware and guided against anything that can steal your joy.

Your happiness is not dependent on anybody because you are enough. Accept and have confidence in yourself. Talk yourself up, and say words like:

"I'm going to live to my fullest potential."

"I'm beautiful."

"I attract opportunity."

"I deserve to take up space."

The positive confessions build confidence in me. I still love helping others, but I must ensure I am ready for it. I have to be in a confident state of mind.

One of the keys to happiness that I have learned to possess is setting boundaries. I let people know what I like and can or cannot tolerate in my relationships. I can choose to do this verbally or with my cations. I ensure that the message is clear.

Another helpful thing is therapy. Therapy allows you to talk to someone else who can see things objectively outside of your regular life. The effect of talking to a professional also makes therapy very effective. A therapist is trained to help and is not judgmental about what you are or may be going through. Anyone can benefit from seeing a therapist. Do not think that you have to have a serious illness to seek help. The reality is that almost anyone, regardless of their mental state and condition, can benefit from therapy.

Get used to accepting sincere compliments from people. Do not just shrug it off. You will not be happy when someone says unkind things about you. Why won't you appreciate someone who does the desirable opposite?

I have learned to connect with the feeling of success, giving myself more praise, more often. Truth is, when someone notices and appreciates something you have done, they are usually being honest. Believe it and take it for what it is. You are great, you are enough. Receive what is well deserved. Never giving up leads you to happiness. You become more motivated to persevere. You eliminate any fears you have experienced. Your emotional intelligence will enhance.

Learn to accept help from others. I have also learned to receive help and not overburden myself. It sounds appealing to tag women as Superwomen, especially those raising children. A superwoman is expected to do everything; go to work, clean the house, cook meals, raise children, take care of the husband, and many more. We are expected to do this. I had to learn to allow others to give. I do not mind. I have learned to relax and let somebody else help me. Many of us find it challenging to get help because we are used to doing things a certain way. Allow yourself to be vulnerable. Feel the love and be grateful. Practice accepting help everywhere. Trying to do everything yourself will eventually take a physical and emotional toll on you, so whenever you need help, just ask for it.

If we cannot add to each other's peace, I do not want it. If it causes me to regress instead of grow, I do not want it.

I know it can be difficult to pinpoint the fine things that are good and bad for you, but pinpointing can clarify the specifics and help you uncover your purpose. And I know all of these things are easier said than done, but to get the best out of what life throws at you, battle those weaknesses and turn them into strengths by taking control and prevailing.

CONQUER YOUR FEAR, SUCCEED, AND WIN....

OVERCOMING SCATTERED SHADOWS

JOURNAL ENTRIES

ONE STEP AT A TIME

OVERCOMING SCATTERED SHADOWS

OBSTACLES
WHAT IS YOUR BIGGEST OBSTACLE THAT YOU'VE HAD TO OVERCOME AND HOW DID YOU DEAL WITH IT?

Notes

Notes

Notes

Notes

Notes

Notes

Notes

Notes

Notes

Notes

Notes

Notes

GOALS

WHAT ARE YOUR SHORT/LONG TERM GOALS AND HOW WOULD YOU ACHIEVE THOSE GOALS?

Notes

Notes

Notes

Notes

Notes

Notes

Notes

Notes

Notes

Notes

Notes

Notes

INSPIRATIONAL WORDS
WHAT WORDS INSPIRE YOU AND GIVE YOU A REASON TO CHALLENGE YOU DAILY?

Notes

Notes

Notes

Notes

Notes

Notes

Notes

Notes

Notes

Notes

Notes

Notes

ACCOMPLISHMENTS

WHAT ARE YOUR ACCOMPLISHMENTS AND ACHIEVEMENTS THAT YOU ARE MOST PROUD OF?; WRITE THEM DOWN AND BE PROUD OF THE PERSON YOU ARE BECOMING.

Notes

Notes

Notes

Notes

Notes

Notes

Notes

Notes

Notes

Notes

Notes

Notes

www.ingramcontent.com/pod-product-compliance
Lightning Source LLC
Chambersburg PA
CBHW022019290426
44109CB00015B/1242